Division of Beat

A Breath Impulse Method For Beginning Band Classes

BOOK 1A

Supplemental Material

By

Harry H. Haines
Music Department Chairman
West Texas State University
Canyon, Texas

And

J. R. McEntyre
Coordinator of Music
Odessa Public Schools
Odessa, Texas

Contributing Editor

Tom C. Rhodes

FINGERING CHART

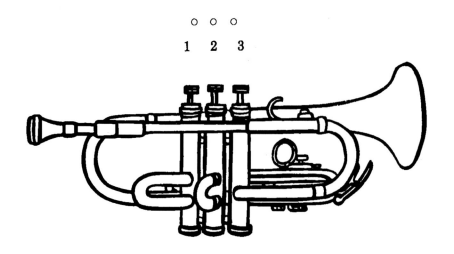

●—means put valve down.   ○—means not to put valve down.

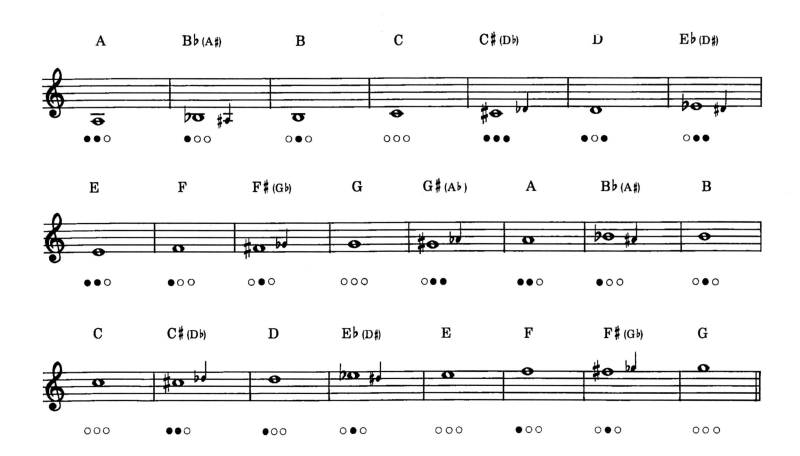

INSTRUMENT POSITION

Embouchure

David Ritter

Suggestions for Trumpet Embouchure are as follows:

1. The corners of the mouth should be firm against the teeth, but not overly tight.

2. The chin should be pointed, but not tense.

3. The jaw should thrust out slightly; the amount of thrust is determined by the individual's over-bite.

4. It is important that the lower lip does not slide under the upper lip.

5. The teeth should be separated slightly, approximately ¼ of an inch.

6. Important!!! The red of the upper and lower lip should be inside the inner rim of the mouthpiece.

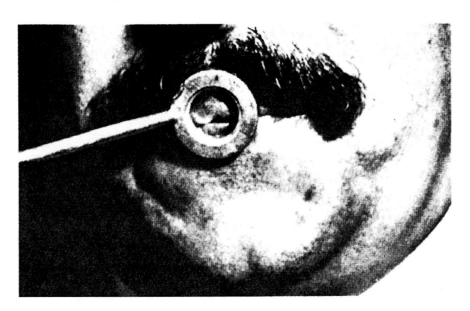

B-323

LESSON 1

Starting on the Mouthpiece

> *This entire lesson is intended as a guide for activities to be explained and demonstrated to the student by the director. While performing, the student is encouraged to watch the director and not the book illustrations. The authors believe that best results will be achieved if the teacher will approach this lesson using a Suzuki-like setting. The basis should be rote teaching using much imitation and repetition.*

I. Buzz a Sound

Start with the mouthpiece in your left hand. Shape your lips as your director explains. Place the mouthpiece in the center of your lips (approximately ⅔ on the upper lip and ⅓ on the lower lip—this may vary somewhat). Look at the picture of the lips and the mouthpiece ring on the previous page. Now, can you make a buzzing sound through the mouthpiece?

Director Buzz   Repeat this many times.   Student Buzz   Try to buzz this sound as long as you can.
(You may want to try to buzz longer than anyone else.)

Try to buzz the same sound as your director:

High Buzz   High Buzz   Low Buzz   Low Buzz
Director Buzz   Student Buzz   Director Buzz   Students Buzz

Now try this siren sound. Can you make the best siren?

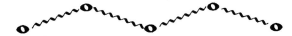

II. Practice Pulsing

To practice pulsing, "hiss" through your teeth very loudly and with great force. Imitate your director. Can you "hiss" louder than your director?

Director:

hiss · ss · ss · ss · ss

Students:

hiss · ss · ss · ss · ss

III. Pulse, the Mouthpiece Sound

Now your director may permit you to Pulse this sound. Try to do this exactly as explained.

Pulse:
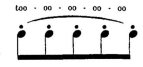
too · oo · oo · oo · oo
Director play

Hold your chin still;
keep the air moving
and the sound going.

Pulse:
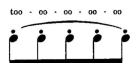
too · oo · oo · oo · oo
Students play

IV. Put It Together

Your director will show you how to hold your instrument. Study the pictures on the previous page.

V. Play Real Notes. Your director will show you how to finger these notes.

G   G   F   F   A   A
Director   Students   Director   Students   Director   Students
Play   Play   Play   Play   Play   Play

Repeat each note many
times in sequence.
DIRECTOR—STUDENT

VI. Tongue a Real Note (Explanation on Page 3)

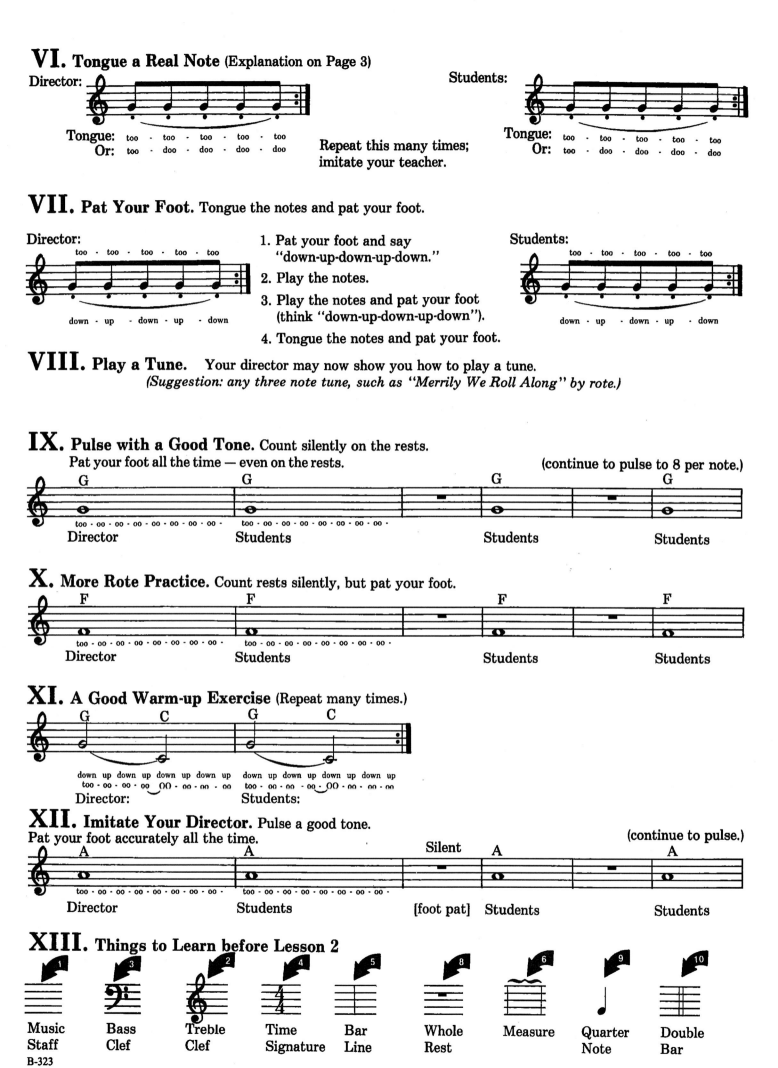

Director:

Tongue: too - too - too - too - too
Or: too - doo - doo - doo - doo

Repeat this many times; imitate your teacher.

Students:

Tongue: too - too - too - too - too
Or: too - doo - doo - doo - doo

VII. Pat Your Foot. Tongue the notes and pat your foot.

Director:

too - too - too - too - too

down - up - down - up - down

1. Pat your foot and say "down-up-down-up-down."
2. Play the notes.
3. Play the notes and pat your foot (think "down-up-down-up-down").
4. Tongue the notes and pat your foot.

Students:

too - too - too - too - too

down - up - down - up - down

VIII. Play a Tune. Your director may now show you how to play a tune.
(Suggestion: any three note tune, such as "Merrily We Roll Along" by rote.)

IX. Pulse with a Good Tone. Count silently on the rests.
Pat your foot all the time — even on the rests.

(continue to pulse to 8 per note.)

G   G   G   G

too - oo - oo - oo - oo - oo - oo - oo -   too - oo - oo - oo - oo - oo - oo - oo -
Director   Students   Students   Students

X. More Rote Practice. Count rests silently, but pat your foot.

F   F   F   F

too - oo - oo - oo - oo - oo - oo - oo -   too - oo - oo - oo - oo - oo - oo - oo -
Director   Students   Students   Students

XI. A Good Warm-up Exercise (Repeat many times.)

G   C   G   C

down up down up down up down up   down up down up down up down up
too - oo - oo - oo oo - oo - oo - oo   too - oo - oo - oo oo - oo - oo - oo
Director: Students:

XII. Imitate Your Director. Pulse a good tone.
Pat your foot accurately all the time.

Silent   (continue to pulse.)

A   A   A   A

too - oo - oo - oo - oo - oo - oo - oo -   too - oo - oo - oo - oo - oo - oo - oo -
Director   Students   [foot pat] Students   Students

XIII. Things to Learn before Lesson 2

| Music Staff | Bass Clef | Treble Clef | Time Signature | Bar Line | Whole Rest | Measure | Quarter Note | Double Bar |

LESSON 2

Suggestion: Start each class with a warm-up using material from lesson 1.

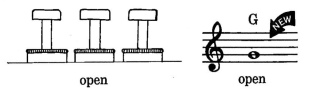

open

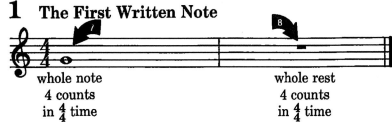

open

Think and Listen!

This symbol denotes something *new!*

Throughout this book, new musical notation and terms are marked with **NEW** sign. The number refers to the Index of Musical terms found on the inside front cover.

1 The First Written Note

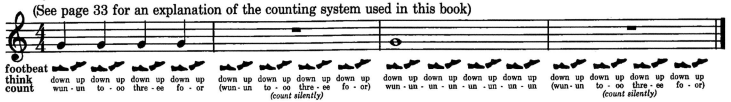

whole note
4 counts
in $\frac{4}{4}$ time

whole rest
4 counts
in $\frac{4}{4}$ time

Repeat this line many times.

2 Add Breath Impulse and Footbeat

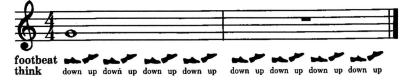

footbeat
think   down up down up down up down up   down up down up down up down up

Play this line many times. Use variations such as teacher play/student play or solo/class.

3 Quarter Notes and Counting

(See page 33 for an explanation of the counting system used in this book)

footbeat
think   down up down up down up down up   down up down up down up down up   down up down up down up down up   down up down up down up down up
count   wun-un to-oo thre-ee fo-or   (wun-un to-oo thre-ee fo-or)   wun-un-un-un-un-un-un-un   (wun-un to-oo thre-ee fo-or)
                                          (count silently)   *(count silently)*

4 Tonguing the Air Stream

too   too   too   too

Right!

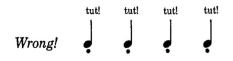

tut!   tut!   tut!   tut!

Wrong!

5 Tonguing Correctly (Smoothly)

footbeat
think   down up down up down up down up   down up down up down up down up   down up down up down up down up   down up down up down up down up
count   wun-un to-oo thre-ee fo-or   wun-un-un-un-un-un-un-un   (wun-un to-oo thre-ee fo-or)   wun-un to-oo thre-ee fo-or
                                                                      (count silently)

6 More Quarter Notes and Whole Notes

footbeat
think   down up down up down up down up   down up down up down up down up   down up down up down up down up   down up down up down up down up
count   wun-un to-oo thre-ee fo-or   (wun-un to-oo thre-ee fo-or)   wun-un to-oo thre-ee fo-or   wun-un-un-un-un-un-un-un)
                                          (count silently)

LESSON 3

It is very important to start each class with a routine to build tone quality.
Suggestion: Use parts IX, X and XI from Lesson 1.

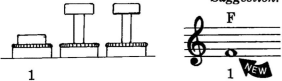

1

7 A Lower Tone

down up down up down up down up   down up down up down up down up   down up down up down up down up   down up down up down up down up
wun-un-un-un-un-un-un-un   (wun-un to-oo three-fo-or)   wun-un to-oo three-e fo-or   wun-un-un-un-un-un-un-un
                                   (count silently)

8 Switcheroo

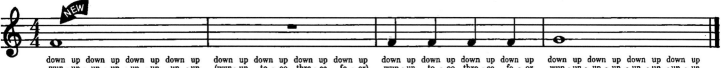

Keep tonguing legato (smoothly).

9 Half Notes and Half Rests

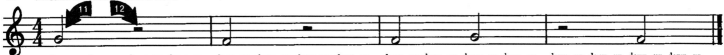

down up down up down up down up   down up down up down up down up   down up down up down up down up   down up down up down up down up
wun-un un-un (thre-ee fo-or)   wun-un-un-un (thre-ee fo-or)   wun-un-un-un three-ee-ee-ee   (wun-un to-oo) thre-ee-ee-ee

10 Who Will Play in the Rest?

down up down up down up down up   down up down up down up down up   down up down up down up down up   down up down up down up down up
wun-un to-oo (thre-ee fo-or)   wun-un to-oo (thre-ee fo-or)   (wun-un to-oo) three-ee fo-or   (wun-un to-oo) three-ee fo-or

11 Quarter Notes and Half Notes

down up down up down up down up   down up down up down up down up   down up down up down up down up   down up down up down up down up
wun-un to-oo three-ee ee-ee   wun-un to-oo (thre-ee fo-or)   wun-un to-oo three-ee ee-ee   wun-un to-oo three-ee ee-ee

12 All Mixed Up!

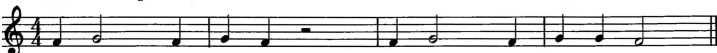

How to become a good player . . . Tap foot, count and play *every* line!

B-323

LESSON 4

Suggestion: Start each class with a warm-up. Use parts IX, X and XI from Lesson 1.

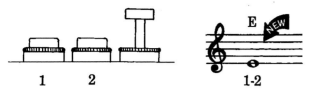

1   2

E **NEW**

1-2

Learn How to Clean Your Instrument Properly.

13 **The Third Note is E** *(ask you teacher about Transposition of instruments.)*

think count   down up down up down up down up   down up down up down up down up   down up down up down up down up   down up down up down up down up
wun-un-un-un-un-un-un-un   (wun-un to-oo thre-ee fo-or)   wun-un to-oo thre-ee fo-or   wun-un-un-un-un-un-un-un
(count silently)

14 **Three Tones Together**

15 **The Echo**

solo   class   solo   class   solo   class   solo   class

16 **Two Lines Together**

Play these lines in unison one at a time, then divide the class and play them as a duet.

down up down up down up down up   down up down up down up down up   down up down up down up down up   down up down up down up down up
wun-un-un-un three-ee-ee-ee   (wun-un to-oo thre-ee fo-or)   wun-un-un-un three-ee-ee-ee   (wun-un to-oo thre-ee fo-or)
(count silently)   *(count silently)*

17

down up down up down up down up   down up down up down up down up   down up down up down up down up   down up down up down up down up
(wun-un to-oo thre-ee fo-or)   wun-un to-oo thre-ee fo-or   (wun-un to-oo thre-ee fo-or)   wun-un to-oo thre-ee fo-or
(count silently)   *(count silently)*

18 **Lots 'O Notes**

Work for legato tonguing style—*long notes.*

19 **Who Will Play in the Rest Again?**

Don't puff out cheeks!

LESSON 5

Suggestion: Add to your warm-up routine line XII from Lesson 1.

20 Going Higher

21 Eighth Notes Are Easy

down up down up down up down up   down up down up down up down up   down up down up down up down up   down up down up down up down up
1   te 2   te 3   te 4   te   wun-un-un-un-un-un-un-un   1   te 2   te 3   te 4   te   wun-un-un-un-un-un-un-un

22 Eighth Notes with Quarter Notes

down up down up down up down up   dotted half   quarter rest
1   te to-oo thre-ee fo-or

23 Tricky Second Count

down up down up down up down up
wun-un 2   te thre-ee fo-or

24 Third Count Mix-Up

down up down up down up down up
wun-un to-oo 3   te fo-or

25 Finally the Fourth Count

down up down up down up down up
wun-un to-oo thre-ee 4   te

Special Assignment: Before going to line #26, try to count and play 1st measures of 22, 23, 24 & 25; then do 2nd measures straight down, then 3rd measures . . . this is a great exercise in rhythm!

26 Rhythmic Challenge

27 Our First Tune

Keep the air flowing; work for legato tonguing style.

B-323

LESSON 6

28 A New High Note

29 Three Beats Per Measure

30 Three-Four Time Again

31 Two Beats Per Measure

32 Counting Notes

33 Counting Rests

34 Hymn Tune

Legato tonguing will help you the most!

B-323

LESSON 7

Suggestion: Start each class with warm-up #1 (Page 28)

35 High Leap

36 Another New Note

37 Twinkle Twinkle This song can be played together with all instruments except B♭ Saxes, Horns, and Oboes.

38 The Tie

39 Play It Again Sam

Repeat Sign

40 Who Will Play on a Rest?

41 Lightly Lightly This line can be played together with all instruments except B♭ Saxes, Horns and Oboes.

Special note to your director: It is suggested that tonguing style now be augmented to include a medium marcato.

B-323

11

LESSON 8

42 Review All Notes

43 Move Those Fingers

down up down up down up down up
wun - un 2 te 3 te 4 te

44 Fingering Mix-Up

down up down up. down up. down up
1 te to - oo 3 te 4 te

45 Fingering Challenge

down up down up down up down up
1 te 2 te thre - ee 4 te

46 Fingering Fight

down up down up down up down up
1 te 2 te 3 te fo - or

Suggestion: As a special assignment, go back and do the 1st measures of lines #43, 44, 45 and 46. Count and then play each "1st measure." Next, count all the 1st measures straight down (without stopping) and then play them straight down. Do the same for the 2nd measures (a ha! the counting isn't written out for you). And finally, count and play the 3rd measures straight down.

47 Dotted Quarter and Eighth Notes

Eighth Notes are sometimes written with a single flag on the stem.

Eighth rest

47-A More Dotted Quarters

48 Dotted Quarter Again

49 Name That Tune

Proper playing position is important.

LESSON 9

50 Playing Lower

51 Clarinet Solo

(clarinets only)

52 Fermata

53 Higher and Lower

54 Moving Up and Down

55 First and Second Endings

56 Jolly Ole St. Nick

57 The Hardest Line (so far)

B-323

LESSON 10
The Key Signature Lesson

58 "The Scale"

59 Another Scale

60 High and Low

61 Last Note Mystery

62 Key Signatures

63 Merrily with a Key Signature

63A Learn a Key Signature Chant

♩ = 60

Key of C,	no flats, no sharps.
Key of G,	1 sharp: F sharp.
Key of D,	2 sharps: F sharp, C sharp.
Key of F,	1 flat: B flat.
Key of B♭,	2 flats: B flat, E flat.
Key of E♭,	3 flats: B flat, E flat, A flat.

(Later, your director will perhaps give you additional chants for other Keys.)

LESSON 11

Suggestion: Add warm-up #2 (Page 28)

64 Slurs and Ties

65 Slurring and Tonguing

66 Clarinets Lower

67 Echo the New Key

68 Is the Echo Correct?

69 Play Lots O'Notes

70 Moving On

71 Marine's Hymn

Fine

D.C. al Fine

Congratulations! You're half-way through the book!

LESSON 12

What Are Keys?

72 Barcarolle in Three Keys

73 Same Song, New Key

74 Again, Another Key

75 Name the Notes (Watch the Key!)

76 More Notes, New Key

77 Say Chant, Name Notes

78 Syncopation

79 Caisson Song

80 (Part of) Our Boys Will Shine

Here's help! On page 30, practice rhythms #43-72. They're lots of fun!

B-323

LESSON 13

81 Going Higher

82 Higher Clarinets

83 Clarinets Higher Still

84 Dedicated to Clarinets

85 Clarinets Sometime Squeak

86 Accompaniment

87 Saints (and pick-up notes)

An incomplete measure?

LESSON 14

88 Slurs

89 Clarinets Can't Play This Now (Later?)

90 Keep It Smooth

Clarinets — right hand down!

91 (Oom) Pa (Oom) Pa

92 Oom (Pa) Oom (Pa)

93 Round

94 Michael Row the Boat Ashore

Are you counting the first two notes correctly?

95 Twinkle Twinkle with Harmony

Fine

D.C. al Fine

B-323

18

LESSON 15
A Time Signature Lesson

A traditional explanation is as follows:

Top Number   = Number of counts in a measure

Bottom Number = The kind of note which receives one count (similar to the bottom
number in reading fractions, 1 = whole note; 2 = half note;
4 = quarter note; 8 = eighth note; etc.)

QUESTIONS: $\frac{4}{4}$ time = __4__ counts per measure, __Quarter__ note receives 1 count.

                $\frac{3}{4}$ time = _____ counts per measure, _____ note receives 1 count.

                $\frac{3}{8}$ time = _____ counts per measure, _____ note receives 1 count.

SUGGESTION: Make up some time signatures and drill for fun!

96 Count and Play

97 For Fun

98 Down in the Valley

99 Row Row th' Boat (Round)

100 East Side-West Side

LESSON 15A
A Time Signature Lesson (continued)
(and a suggested new way to explain time signatures)

The time signatures listed on the previous page are explained in terms of their traditional definitions. (Sometimes this is referred to as "simple time.") A lot of music today, however, makes it necessary to explain time signatures in a different way. One different way to do this is to group three eighth notes into one beat (example: ♪♪♪ = ♩., so a dotted quarter becomes the note that gets a beat in fast ⅜ time.) Combining several counts into one larger beat is sometimes called "compound time." For this reason, it is important that you learn a different way to understand time signatures. It is as follows:

Traditional
Explanation: ⅜ = 3 counts per measure and an eighth note receives 1 count.

Different
Explanation: ⅜ = 3 eighth notes or their equivalent in each full measure.

Does this help? Try it out to see how it actually works! For each of the lines on this page (which may sound *very* familiar) try to tap your foot, count and play using only one beat per measure, three breath impulses per beat. The counts have been written under the first few measures to help you. You may have more fun and these lines might sound even better to you played one beat per measure.

Now play this entire page in one count per measure.

96A **Count and Play** this way (in one)

97A **For Fun**

98A **Down in the Valley**

99A **Row Row th' Boat (Round)**

100A **East Side-West Side**

LESSON 16
Suggestion: Add warm-up #3 (Page 28)

Dynamics: Can You Name 6 Levels?

pp p mp mf f ff

101 A♭ Concert Scale in ⅜ Time

mf

Can you count and play this 2 ways?

102 A♭ Concert Scale in ¾ Time

f

Can you count and play this 2 ways?

> *Suggestion: Now go back to Lesson 6 and play through the book again counting and playing all ¾ lines one beat per measure. You'll be surprised how quickly you can do this (and how much better many lines sound when played fast!).*

103 Dear, Dear! ♩.= 60

melody

mf

accompaniment

p

104 Dona Nobis Pacem ♩= 60

p

Some lines will always sound better when played slowly.

SUPPLEMENTAL LESSON I

The "Waltz Time" Lesson

Book 1

A. Scale in ³⁄₈ Time ♩.= 60

B. Scale in Waltz Time ♩.= 60

C. Round in Waltz Time ♩.= 60

D. Bear Went O'er the Mountain ♩.= 60

E. Sweet Betsy From Pike

melody

accompaniment

B323

SUPPLEMENTAL LESSON II
Some lines with Two Impulses
Some lines with Three Impulses

F. Duet (Part 1)

G. Duet (Part 2)

H. Helping Clarinets

I. More Help For Clarinets

J. Band Played On ♩.= 60

K. Sidewalks of New York

melody

accompaniment

SUPPLEMENTAL LESSON III
Reviewing the Dotted Quarter Note

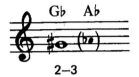

L. America (♩ = 60; 3 beats per measure)

M. Dotted Quarter Notes

N. The First Beat

O. The Second Beat

P. The Third Beat

Q. West Texas Song

SUPPLEMENTAL LESSON IV
Building Range and Technique

R. Duet (Part 1)

S. Duet (Part II)

T. Basic Technique

U. Building Technique

V. On Top of Ole Smoky (♩.=60, in one)

W. East Side, West Side ♩.=60

LESSON 17

105 Db Concert Scale in 3/8 Time

106 Db Concert Scale in 6/8 Time

107 Chopsticks

mf

mf

107A Triplets

108 Pop Goes the Weasel

f

Pop!

109 Dotted Half 1 Count

♩.=60

1 lah lee 1 un un

110 Dotted Half 2 Counts

♩.=60

1 lah lee 2 lah lee 1 un un un un un

111 Dotted Half 3 Counts

♩.=60

1 te 2 te 3 te 1 un un un un un

112 Our Director March

solo

accompaniment

It is very important that you use warm-up #3 to practice every day playing four impulses per beat.

B-323

26

LESSON 18

113 Chromatic Scale in ⅜

114 Chromatic Scale in 9⁄8

115 Beautiful Dreamer

116 Enharmonic

Ask your teacher about "E to F" and "B to C", then write some enharmonic notes.

117 Sharps Ascending, Flats Descending

118 Looby Loo

119 Carnival of Venice

120 Good Night Ladies

Andante

LESSON 19

> *Suggestion: A really great way to review fundamentals and practice playing cut time (at the same time) is to go back through this book playing all of the $\frac{4}{4}$ lines (that do not include 8th notes) twice as fast... as though they were written in cut time. You'll be surprised how quickly you can play these lines and it will probably help your ego to see how much you've improved.*

122 Football Tune

Allegro

123 Beethoven's 9th

Maestoso

124 Palo Duro Canyon March

mf

LESSON 20

125 **Technique Fun**

126 **Technique Fun Lil' Harder**

127 **Harder 'N Harder**

128 **Hardest Line in the Book?**

129 **Stars and Stripes Forever**

130 **Long, Long Ago**

Practice "more rhythms" on page 31 — this will help you even more.

B-323

LESSON 21

Suggestion: Add warm-up #4 (Page 28)

131 Sixteenth Notes Have Finally Arrived

132 More Sixteenths

133 Love Those Sixteenths

134 Sixteenths Forever

135 Ten Little Indians

136 Little Brown Jug

137 Dixie (Is Too Hard for This Book?)

This line is too difficult for this book. Can you play it?

B-323

LESSON 22

138 **Running Sixteenths**

139 **Same Thing in Cut Time**

THE BIG PAY-OFF!! *Now that you can count and play 8th notes in cut time (which are really sixteenth notes . . . right!) go back through the book and play all of the* 4/4 *lines which contain 8th notes and do them in cut time. Tap foot, count and play every line; you'll be an expert in DIVISION OF BEAT!*

140 **William Tell**
Allegro

141 **Hi Ho, Nobody Home (Round)**

142 **Aura Lee**
Andante

mp

B-323 mf

SUGGESTED WARM-UPS

Note: These should be memorized as quickly as possible and played as a daily routine at the beginning of each class session.

Warm-up 1 (For lessons 7-22) Two breath impulses per ♩ = 60

Warm-up 2 (For lessons 11-22) Three breath impulses per beat ♩. = 60

Warm-up 3 (For lessons 16-22) Four breath impulses per beat ♩ = 60

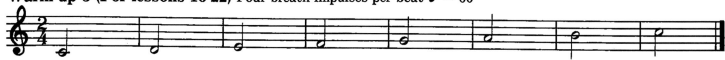

Warm-up 4 (For lessons 21-22) Six breath impulses per beat ♩. = 60

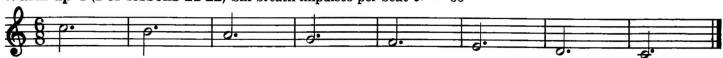

Suggestion: As soon as practical, change warm-ups 1 and 2 above to chromatic and delete rests.

Warm-up 5 (For introduction to Book II)

B-323

32

Hi Ho
A special solo with piano accompaniment

Bb Trumpet/Cornet

Arr. B. G. Evans

RHYTHM EXERCISE
Set 1
(All exercises on this page can be counted with 2 impulses)

*Exercises 73-84 should also be counted one beat per measure using three pulses.

You could be tested on some of these rhythms.   34

B-323

RHYTHM EXERCISE
Set 2
(For 3 impulses and 4 impulses)

SPECIAL SONGS FOR INDIVIDUAL PRACTICE

Note: This is not a unison page. Songs will vary from instrument to instrument.

Up On the Housetop

America the Beautiful

Red River Valley

Taps

Reveille

Musical Terms Index

1 **Staff**—5 lines and 4 spaces.

2 **Treble Clef Sign**

3 **Bass Clef Sign**

4 $\frac{4}{4}$ **Time Signature**
  a—4 beats in each measure.
  b—each ♩ note gets one beat.

5 **Bar**—Divides staff into measures.

6 **Measure**—Space between two bars.

6A ♭ **Flat**—Lowers a tone ½ step.

6B ♯ **Sharp**—Raises a tone ½ step.

6C ♮ **Natural**—Indicates that the note is not to be sharped or flatted. It cancels the effect of a sharp or flat.

7 o **Whole Note**

8 **Whole Rest**

9 ♩ **Quarter Note**

10 **Double Bar**—Marks the end of a section.

11 ♩ **Half Note**

12 **Half Rest**

13 ♫ **Eighth Notes**

14 ♩. **Dotted Half Note**

15 𝄽 **Quarter Rest**

16 $\frac{3}{4}$ **Time Signature**
  a—3 beats in each measure
  b—each ♩ note gets one beat.

16-A $\frac{2}{4}$ **Time Signature**
  a—2 beats in each measure
  b—each ♩ note gets one beat.

17 **Tie**—Combines two or more notes of the same pitch

18 **Repeat Dots**—Repeat entire section.

19 ♩. **Dotted Quarter Note**

20 **Hold or Fermata**—Give extra time.

21 **1st and 2nd Endings**
Play 1st ending the first time then repeat strain and play 2nd ending.

22 **Key Signature**—Flats or sharps placed at the beginning of a section, indicate that these notes are sharped or flatted throughout the section.

23 **Slur**—Different pitches joined by a curved line in which only the first note is tongued.

24 *Fine*—Finish

25 *D.C. al Fine*—Go back to the beginning and play until you come to *Fine*.

26 𝄾 **Eighth Rest**

27
  pp —very soft
  p —soft
  mp —moderately soft
  mf —moderately loud
  f —loud
  ff —very loud

28 ∕. Repeat the preceding measure.

29 **Pick Up Notes**—An incomplete measure at the beginning; note values are usually taken from the last measure.

30 C **Time Signature**—This means common time which is the same as $\frac{4}{4}$ Time.

31 **Andante**—Moderately slow and smooth flowing.

32 **Allegro**—Quite fast.

33 **Maestoso**—Majestically.

34 ¢ **Cut Time**—Same as $\frac{2}{2}$ time. Means to cut all note values to half as long.

35 **Sixteenth Notes**

36 **Sixteenth Rest**

37 **Accompaniment**—A part that supports the melody but is subordinate to it.

38 **Enharmonic**—Two different names for one tone.

39 , **Breath Mark.**

*EASTMAN SYSTEM OF COUNTING (Simplified)

I. Notes of one or more counts

Notes of one count (or longer) are counted much the same way as any counting system; simply say the number of the count on which the note begins and continue the word-sound for the duration of the note. Thus a note which receives one count and which begins on the first beat of the measure would be counted "one"; if it were on the second count, say "two," etc. A note of longer value would simply be held longer; thus a whole note (in $\frac{4}{4}$ time) would be counted "onnnnnnnnnne" for 4 counts. This has the advantage of making the verbalization most nearly approximate the sound of an instrument playing the actual rhythm and requires the identical mental process of thinking the number of counts while a continuous sound is produced. The following example quickly illustrates Eastman Counting as applied to rhythms (including rests) of 1, 2, 3 or 4 counts.

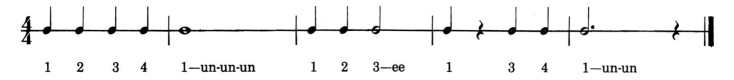

1   2   3   4   1—un-un-un   1   2   3—ee   1   3   4   1—un-un

II. Counting the sub-divisions

Notes which receive less than a full count are divided into rhythms which are divisable by 2 and those which are divisable by 3 (some would say duple and triple rhythms). Again, any note which occurs on a downbeat is simply counted with the number of the count; the important difference is that a note which occurs the last ½ of a count is counted "te" (latin, rhymes with May) and notes which occur on the second ⅓ of the count and last ⅓ of the count are counted "lah" and "lee."

Rhythms which are divisable by 2

1   te

Rhythms which are divisable by 3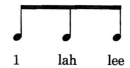

1   lah   lee

III. *Everything* else is counted "Ta"

1 ta te ta

1 ta lah ta lee ta

1   te ta

1   lah ta lee ta

1 ta te

1 ta lah ta lee

1   ta

1   ta lee

*For the complete explanation of this counting system, see *Ear Training and Sight Singing Dictation Manual* by Alan I. McHose, published by Prentice Hall.

B-323

Selected Trumpet Publications

METHODS

IRONS, EARL

B114   27 Groups Of Exercises for Trumpet   HL3770191

Trumpet players/students around the world rely on this collection of studies for the development of embouchure, lip flexibility , breath control and extraordinary tonguing techniques that provide a strong base for improved performance and endurance.

SOLO WITH PIANO

ANDRAUD, ALBERT J.

Mager, Georges

B117   Nine Grand Solos de Concert   HL3770195

One of the key repertoire collections for any trumpet player. It features many of the standard solo repertoire demanded by serious trumpet player/students.Includes: Solo de Concert-Hue; Concertino-Senee; Morceau de Concours-Savard; Solo de Concert-Erlanger; Fantasie-Thome; Andante and Allegretto-Balay; Andante and Allegro-Ropartz; Petite Piece Concertante-Balay; Concert Polonaise for two trumpets-Rougnon.

BALAY, GUILLAUME

Andraud, Albert J.

SS143   Andante and Allegretto   HL3773747

Revised by Georges C. Mager and Albert J. Andraud. For Trumpet or Cornet.

BALAY, GUILLAUME

Mager, Georges

SS300   Petite Piece Concertante   HL3773927

BELLSTEDT, HERMAN

Simon, Frank/ Fry, Tommy J.

SS310   Napoli   HL3773938

Napoli is perhaps the most famous solo by Sousa arranger and cornet virtuoso Hermann Bellstedt. Conceived as a theme and variations on a wildly popular 19th Century song, this edition for trumpet and piano was collated by Bellstedt's student and Sousa band successor Frank Simon. Arrangements for trumpet and piano, trombone and piano, and trumpet or trombone and full orchestra are also available from the publisher.

EWAZEN, ERIC

SU445   Ballade for a Ceremony (A Marriage Ballade)   HL3776363

Was commissioned by Jason Adams as a gift for his friend, Matthew Bickel, in celebration of Matthew's marriage to Christine Sodero Bickel. Trumpet parts in both Bb and C are provided.

SU337   Concerto No. 1 for Trumpet (Sonata No. 1)   HL3776234

Commissioned by the International Trumpet Guild, recorded by Chris Gekker on Well-Tempered Productions. Ca. 20'. Later expanded into an orchestra concerto, also available from the publisher.

SU397   Concerto No. 2 for Trumpet and Strings (reduction)   HL3776299

Quintet for Trumpet and Strings was commissioned by and dedicated to Chris Gekker, who premiered the work at the International Trumpet Guild convention in College Park, Maryland in May of 1991. The work was later set with full string orchestra with the title "Concerto No. 2 for Trumpet and Strings". Both versions, as well as a trumpet/ piano reduction are available from the publisher.

SU512   Prayer and Praise   HL3776433

EWAZEN, ERIC

Gekker, Chris

SU518   A Hymn for the Lost and the Living (trumpet solo)   HL3776438

After witnessing the tragic aftermath of the September 11, 2001 attack on New York firsthand, Ewazen composed this as a memorial to those who lost their lives, and as a tribute to the resilience and determination of those left behind. This arrangement for trumpet and piano is by trumpeter Chris Gekker. (2002) Ca. 9'

FITZGERALD, BERNARD

Fitzgerald, Bernard

ST189   Ballad   HL3774787

GOEYENS, ALPHONSE

SS319   All 'antica   HL3773947

IRONS, EARL

SS73   Song Of the Pines for Trumpet   HL3774390

Can be played on Bb trumpet, cornet, or tenor saxophone.

REED, ALFRED

SS756   Ode for Trumpet   HL3774418

This early masterpiece of Alfred Reed first appeared as a 1956 wind band edition published by Charles Hanson Music with a condensed score only. In recognition of Reed's position as one of the most important composers of serious music for wind band, Southern Music prepared a full score to the piece on the 30th anniversary of their publication. Available accompaniments from the publisher include full orchestra and piano in addition to the wind (concert) band version. Dedicated to trumpeter Don Jacoby who premiered the work at TMEA 1956.

ROPARTZ, J. GUY

Andraud, Albert J.

SS322   Andante and Allegro   HL3773950

An early twentieth French composer, Ropartz' music is well regarded for its logic, clarity, and lack of excessive material.

SOLOMON, EDWARD

Solomon, Edward

B396   Trumpet Solos for the Young Player   HL3770602

These twelve solos for young trumpet players are each written in a different style, offering an opportunity early in the development of a player to focus on elements of musicality. Songs include: I. The Bugle, II. Country Dance, III. Crossroads, IV. A Little Solo, V. Marching Song, VI. A Minor Etude, VII. A Modest Mazurka, VIII. Polka Time, IX. Someday, X. Miniminuet, XI. Trumpeter's Hymn, XII. Summer Breeze

TELEMANN, GEORG PHILLIPP

Chidester, L.W.

ST103   Andante and Presto   HL3774694

VIZZUTTI, ALLEN

SU522   Sonata No. 2   HL3776445

This Sonata for trumpet and piano was composed without extremes of range, technique or endurance to enhance the repertoire for trumpet players of all ages. Set in the standard sonata form of three movements (I. Moderato, II. Andante, III. Allegro), it is a melodic piece with contemporary flair. Our hope is that it will be fun to perform, enjoyable to hear, and serious enough to express one's self musically.

QUARTET

BACH, J.S.

Thurston, Richard

SU124   Jesu, Joy of Man's Desiring   HL3775944

A beautiful arrangement of one of Bach's most well-down melodies written as a quartet. Versions by Richard Thurston available from the publisher for other instrument quartets include: Flute, Clarinet, Saxophone (AATB), Trumpet, Horn, Tuba, Violin, Viola, and Cello

Exclusively distributed by

Questions/ comments? info@laurenkeisermusic.com

SELECTED CONTEMPORARY TRUMPET SOLOS

BALENTINE, JAMES
SU377   Prayer And Alleluia   HL3776281

BARNES, JAMES
SU296   Fanfare and Capriccio, Op. 102   HL3776179
(reduction)

Written for trumpeter Allen Vizzuti, this edition for piano and trumpet includes both the original solo part and a version as performed by Allen Vizzuti. (1999) ca. 8'.

BELLSTEDT, HERMAN
SS99   Echoes Of Willow Grove   HL3774681

BERIOT, CHARLES-AUGUSTE DE
SS315   Scene De Ballet   HL3773943

BEVERSDORF, THOMAS
SS144   Sonata   HL3773748

BORDNER, GERALD
ST835   Dramatic Waltz   HL3775669

CAMPBELL, BRUCE
ST910   Procession (Bb or C trumpet)   HL3775766

ERLANGER, CAMILLE
SS113   Solo De Concert   HL3773713

EWAZEN, ERIC
SU445   Ballade for a Ceremony   HL3776363

SU337   Concerto No. 1 for Trumpet (Sonata No.   HL3776234
1)

Commissioned by the International Trumpet Guild, recorded by Chris Gekker on Well-Tempered Productions. Ca. 20'. Later expanded into an orchestra concerto, also available from the publisher.

SU397   Concerto No. 2 for Trumpet and Strings   HL3776299
(reduction)

Quintet for Trumpet and Strings was commissioned by and dedicated to Chris Gekker, who premiered the work at the International Trumpet Guild convention in College Park, Maryland in May of 1991. The work was later set with full string orchestra with the title "Concerto No. 2 for Trumpet and Strings". Both versions, as well as a trumpet/ piano reduction are available from the publisher.

SU512   Prayer and Praise   HL3776433

FITZGERALD, BERNARD
ST189   Ballad   HL3774787

ST161   Burlesca   HL3774756

GIOVANNINI, CAESAR
ST675   Romance   HL3775445

GOEYENS, ALPHONSE
SS319   All 'antica   HL3773947

HAACK, PAUL
ST641   Jive Five   HL3775406

IRONS, EARL
SS73   Song Of The Pines   HL3774390

JARVIS, DAVID E.
SU271   Macbeth And Macdonwald   HL3776144

KOCH, FREDERICK
ST962   Three Impressions   HL3775848

KREISLER, ALEXANDER VON
SS721   Sonatina   HL3774380

REED, ALFRED
SS756   Ode For Trumpet   HL3774418

ROUSE, STEVE
X221001   The Avatar   HL41594

A three movement solo for trumpet doubling on flugelhorn and piccolo trumpet. Recorded by Raymond Mase on Summit Records DCD 148.

SCHUDEL, THOMAS
ST989   Serenade   HL3775895

SENEE, HENRI
SS111   Concertino   HL3773712

SIMON, FRANK
SS323   Miss Bluebonnet   HL3773951

SOLOMON, EDWARD
ST611   Ballade In D Minor   HL3775365

ST705   Dance Suite   HL3775492

SU133   Solitary Trumpet   HL3775954

ST501   Trumpet Of Castille   HL3775215

UBER, DAVID
ST572   Ecnamor (Romance)   HL3775308

VIZZUTTI, ALLEN
SU522   Sonata No. 2   HL3776445

WALTERS, DAVID
ST357   Andante And Scherzo   HL3775013

SS902   Episode   HL3774585

WEINER, LAWRENCE
ST628   Suite   HL3775385

WIENANDT, ELWYN
ST654   Two Short Pieces   HL3775417

WOODBURY, ARTHUR
SU184   Homage To Erik   HL3776020

Exclusively distributed by  HAL•LEONARD® CORPORATION

Questions/ comments? info@laurenkeisermusic.com